The Illustrated Story of President

HAROLD B. LEE

Great Leaders of The Church
of Jesus Christ of Latter-day Saints

The Illustrated Story of President Harold B. Lee
Great Leaders of The Church of Jesus Christ
of Latter-day Saints

Copyright © 1982 by
Eagle Systems International
P.O. Box 508
Provo, Utah 84603

ISBN: 0-938762-11-7
Library of Congress Catalog Card No.: 82-70685

Fourth Printing April 1987

First Edition

All rights reserved. No part of this publication may be reproduced or used in any manner or by any means—graphic, electronic, or mechanical, including photocopying, recording, taping, or information storage and retrieval systems—without written permission of the publisher.

Lithographed in U.S.A.
by
COMMUNITY PRESS, INC.

A Member of
The American Bookseller's Association
New York, New York

The Illustrated Story of President

HAROLD B. LEE

Great Leaders of The Church of Jesus Christ of Latter-day Saints

We thank the family of Harold B. Lee for their generous help and cooperation in this project.

AUTHOR Lucille Reading	**ADVISORS AND EDITORS** Paul & Millie Cheesman
ILLUSTRATOR B. Keith Christensen	Mark Ray Davis L. Norman Egan
DIRECTOR AND CORRELATOR Lael J. Woodbury	Annette Hullinger Beatrice W. Friel

PUBLISHER
Steven R. Shallenberger

A Biography Of
HAROLD B. LEE

Harold Bingham Lee was born on March 28, 1899, in Clifton, Idaho. He was the second child born to Samuel Marion and Louisa Emeline Bingham Lee. On Sunday, June 9, 1907, Harold was baptized in a pond near his home and then confirmed a member of The Church of Jesus Christ of Latter-day Saints.

As a boy, Harold was a good student who loved to read, and throughout his life he was involved in some aspect of education. After graduating from Albion State Normal School at age seventeen, he taught grades one through eight at Silver Star School near Weston, Idaho. Only one year later he became principal of the district school at Oxford, Idaho, and years later he was appointed principal of two schools in the Granite School District in Salt Lake City, Utah.

When Harold B. Lee was twenty-one, he was called to the Western States Mission. Sixteen months of his mission he acted as president of the Denver Conference. When he returned from his mission, he moved to Salt Lake City to continue his education. On November 14, 1923, he married Fern Lucinda Tanner in the Salt Lake Temple.

The years between 1930 and 1937 Harold B. Lee served as President of the Pioneer Stake in Salt Lake City. In addition he was appointed as one of the Salt Lake City Commissioners. While serving as stake president, he instituted a welfare program in his stake made necessary by the depression of the 1930's. The leaders of the Church were pleased with this program, and on April 20, 1935, Brother Lee was called as managing director of the Church Welfare Program. In this capacity he worked with others, expanding and extending welfare services throughout the Church.

Six years later, on April 10, 1941, Harold B. Lee was ordained an apostle by President Heber J. Grant. He served as a member of the Quroum of the Twelve for the next thirty-one years.

Elder Lee received honorary doctor's degrees from Utah State University and the University of Utah. In addition he received the Silver Buffalo from the Boy Scouts of America in 1963.

Elder Lee was active in the business community and served as a member of numerous boards of directors, including: American Red Cross, Equitable Life Assurance Society, Union Pacific Railroad, and chairman of the board of Zion's First National Bank.

In 1962 Elder Lee's wife, Fern, died. This brought him much sorrow and loneliness, and the following year on June 17, 1963, he married his second wife, Freda Joan Jensen, in the Salt Lake Temple.

In 1970 Elder Lee was set apart as First Counselor to President Joseph Fielding Smith, and in 1972 he delivered the dedicatory prayers at the Ogden and Provo temples. On July 7, 1972, Harold B. Lee was ordained the eleventh President of The Church of Jesus Christ of Latter-day Saints.

President Lee was a well-educated man, dedicated to uplifting and blessing the lives of others. He once said, "It is what you and I give to others that means more than all the sermons we preach; the lessons of our lives, the sermon of our own conduct and our own character will be most powerful in helping others."

After serving seventeen months as president, Harold B. Lee died on December 26, 1973, at the age of seventy-four.

Spring had not come into bloom in Clifton, Idaho, on March 28, 1899, but there was more than a hint of promise in the nearby mountains and in the yard around the home of Samuel Marion and Louisa Emeline Bingham Lee. Inside the farmhouse there was far more than a hint of promise, as Louisa cradled her second child, a newborn son, in her arms.

Harold Bingham Lee recorded the event in his journal many years later: "There seems to have been some disappointment when I arrived, Mother having hoped for a girl."

But if Harold's mother felt even a tinge of disappointment because her new child was a boy, it was only momentarily.

One hot summer evening Harold was seated and playing before the open kitchen door with his mother, grandmother, and two or three of the younger children.

Brilliant zigzag flashes of lightning streaked across the dark sky and, at almost the same time, breathtaking thunder crackled and crashed around the mountains. The storm was fierce and the family drew close as they watched the brilliant display.

Suddenly without warning, his mother gave Harold a vigorous push that sent him sprawling on his back onto the floor. At that instant a bolt of lightning came down the chimney of the kitchen stove, out through the open doorway, and split a huge gash from top to bottom in a large tree immediately in front of the house.

"Whew!" Harold may have exclaimed. "If you hadn't pushed me out of the way, I'd have been struck by that lightning." Had it not been for his Mother's intuitive act, he would not have lived to fulfill his destiny as a Church leader.

Years later Harold must have walked out and looked in amazement at the deep lightning scar on that large tree. He probably stood for a reverent and prayerful moment. Then speaking from a grateful heart, he said, "I thank Thee, Lord, for that precious gift possessed in abundant measure by my mother."

One morning shortly after this time, Harold and his mother were alone in their home. "Harold," she called, "I'm making soap and I need that large tub of lye on the high shelf. Can you help me?"

"Yes, Mother," he replied. He climbed on a chair and began to carefully lift down the tub. It was exactly above Harold's head when his hold slipped and the strong lye poured over the boy's head, face, and arms.

With almost superhuman speed his mother kicked off the lid of a jar of pickled beets she had just made. With her cupped hands she dipped out the reddened pickle vinegar and poured it over her son's burning skin to stop the eating of the lye.

As the liquid eased the pain, he may have moaned softly, "Oh, that helps. Thank you, Mother." Then he lay quietly while Louisa offered a fervent prayer for his comfort and complete recovery from the searing burns. Again her prayers in his behalf were quickly answered.

One day Harold went with his father to the fields. Just over the fence to the east of their property on some neighboring land were several old sheds and barns that had blown down. "What a wonderful place to explore," Harold thought, parting the wires so he could crawl through the fence.

Just as he did so he heard a quiet, clear voice, say distinctly, "Harold, don't go near that lumber over there!"

He looked around to see if his father had spoken, but his father was far off in the field. The startled boy wondered where the voice had come from. He saw no one, but he did not question the warning. Quickly he turned and ran as fast as possible away from the unknown danger. In recalling this and other marvelous experiences he said, "How thankful I was for that warning. Throughout my childhood there seemed to be a guiding hand over me!"

Years later when Harold was in high school, his mother's sensitivity to him and to the Spirit was again evident. Harold was a debator and a very important meet was to be held. "We haven't a chance of winning," he might have declared, then adding, "but we must! It doesn't make any sense, Mother."

"Of course, it makes sense, dear," she replied. "And I'm sure everything will be just fine."

And everything was just fine as far as Harold was concerned, for his team won every one of its debates. Excited with the way the meet had turned out, he telephoned his mother to tell her. "We won, we won!" he shouted into the phone.

"I know, dear," she answered. "And when you get home, I'll tell you all about it."

When Harold arrived home, Louisa took her son aside and made this simple explanation: "When I knew it was just time for your debate to start, I went out among the willows by the creek side and prayed to God that you would not fail. There I received assurance that you would not."

One stormy night when her son was late getting home, Louisa paced the floor uneasily. "You must go and see where Harold is," she urged her husband. "I know something has happened to him and he needs your help."

Samuel knew better than to disregard the spiritual promptings of his sensitive wife. He put on his clothing, tucked a warm blanket under his arm, and went out into the freezing night to look for Harold. He found him bruised, cold, and caked with half-frozen mud. Harold's horse had stumbled while crossing a stream and he was thrown into a pond. As Samuel wrapped his son in the blanket, Harold said gratefully, "I'm so glad you came. How did you know I needed help?"

"It was your mother's idea," Samuel replied. "She always knows."

"Thank you," the young man said as his father wrapped the quilt around his muddy body. Then he whispered quietly, "And I thank Thee, Father, for letting my mother know I needed help and for bringing my father here."

Years ago, before Harold was old enough to go to school, he had pleaded: "Please, let me go to school with my brother Perry."

Finally his mother told him, "You may go with Perry this morning if you promise to be a good boy and sit quietly so you won't disturb the other children."

The school was two miles away, but the two little boys had grown strong from work around the farm, and they eagerly ran off together. The school teacher, Chloe McNeil Howell, knew the boys, for she was also their Sunday School teacher. She welcomed them warmly, then gave Harold some crayons to play with while she went on with the regular lessons.

Quietly the little boy bent over his work. He was so absorbed in what he was doing that sometime later the teacher went to the back of the room to see what he was doing. "Why, Harold," she exclaimed in surprise, "You've written all your A B C's and your name! You should be in school all of the time. I'll speak to your mother about it."

Louisa consented to the teacher's suggestion that Harold become a regular student, even though it placed him two years ahead of his age group. His days there were filled with the excitement of learning. For many years after that memorable first day of school, he was associated in some way with schools in Idaho and Utah.

When he was only seventeen, Harold became teacher-principal of the one-room Silver Star School located near Weston, Idaho. He taught all of the grades one through eight. He was younger than several of the boys in the school, but they didn't know it—and he saw no need to tell them!

The following year he became principal of the district school at Oxford, Idaho. Some years later he served as principal to two different schools in Salt Lake County.

All his life Harold loved books and learning. He often recalled the first book he ever owned and the events surrounding his being given this treasure. It was Christmas Eve and all the boys and girls of Clifton excitedly gathered for the community Christmas tree party. The huge tree was aglow with hundreds of burning candles. One of the men from the town, dressed as Santa Claus, came ho-ho-hoing into the hall where the party was being held. Somehow he got too close to the flames and his cotton beard caught fire.

The children, horrified, started to scream as the man frantically ran out through a rear exit. Along with him went the tree trimmings, candles, presents, and even a part of the tree itself.

Someone else took Santa's place to distribute the rest of the gifts, but nothing was found that had Harold's name written on it. The sad little boy hurried home by himself.

"Why didn't you stay at the party?" his father asked.

"Is something wrong?" his mother questioned.

With tears running down his face, Harold explained, "Santa Claus caught on fire, most of the tree burned down, and there wasn't any present for me."

His parents comforted him as well as they could and helped him into bed. The next day the man who cleaned up after the Christmas Eve fire came unexpectedly to the Lee home. In his hand he carried a half burned book entitled "Tom, the Bootblack," and written inside was the name Harold B. Lee. Many books were owned by Harold during his lifetime, but none were received with more joy than this very first one.

"Living as a boy at the foot of a great mountain in a valley surrounded by mountains," he recalled, "It was probably to be expected that stories of the outdoors and of animals were particularly appealing. I read every book I could get my hands on. One I particularly remember was *Adventures of a Grizzly*."

Many years later, in talking with a friend about the joys of reading, he said, "It is wonderful to me just to hold a good book in my hands, to feel its cover, to trace the imprinted words on a page with my fingers, and to know that the riches of reading are waiting for me there."

On the beautiful Sunday morning of June 9, 1907, Harold was baptized and confirmed a member of the Church. The place chosen for this sacred ordinance was a picturesque pond at an old lime kiln in Clifton, Idaho. This was on the property of a neighbor of the Lee family. Thus began his membership in the Church that someday he would lead as its president.

Harold Bingham Lee became the eleventh President of The Church of Jesus Christ of Latter-day Saints on Friday, July 7, 1972. This seemed in direct fulfillment of promises made to him in his patriarchal blessing given in March, 1917: "It is thy privilege to do a great work on the earth. . . . If thou art prayerful and humble, thou shalt labor in places of great responsibility, in presiding among the people with whom thou art located."

Harold's father was bishop of the ward where he received his mission call. He was asked to serve the Lord in what was then the Western States Mission. While there he served for sixteen months as president of the Denver Conference.

Soon after his return home, Harold moved to Salt Lake City, Utah, to further his education, completing it through correspondence and extension courses and by attending summer school.

Almost as soon as Harold settled in Salt Lake City, he became active in leadership positions in the Church. He was ward M Men leader, stake Sunday school superintendent, a member of the high council, a counselor in the stake presidency, and from 1930 to 1937, he served as president of the Pioneer Stake. He also taught seminary part-time during these years.

His performance in all of these positions and the many more to which he was called showed not only his great leadership but also the rare compassion that he exemplified all his life.

The first Christmas he was stake president, his two little girls happily took their new dolls to a home of one of their friends to show their lovely gifts. They soon came home, tears welling in their eyes.

"What in the world is the matter?" the anxious parents asked their sobbing daughters. They answered, "They didn't have Christmas at their house!" Suddenly they both realized that the father of the girls' friend had been out of work Undoubtedly there was no money for Christmas gifts.

That night as President Lee knelt in prayer, he promised the Lord that as long as he was in that stake, he would make sure that every family there had some kind of Christmas dinner and some Christmas gifts for every Christmas thereafter. He solemnly vowed, "God grant that I will never let another year pass but that I, as a leader, will truly know my people. I will know their needs, I will be conscious of those who most need my leadership, and I will help them."

Thousands alive today can testify that this pledge made on that Christmas night was kept until President Lee's dying day—he kept it personally as well as in his calling as a leader of the Church. Before Christmas came again, he had called together all of the bishops and the ward and stake leaders. They made plans to provide for the 4,800 needy stake members, including about 1,000 children under the age of ten years, so that they all could have Christmas in their homes.

The next year at Christmastime a heavy snow fell in the area. The night before Christmas Eve, President Lee, who had been appointed Street Commissioner at this time, was out all night helping the road crews clear the city streets. As he was driving to his office the next day, he saw a little boy on the roadside hitchhiking. He saw that the child had no coat, gloves, nor overshoes. He stopped.

"I'm on my way into town," he called. "Would you like to ride with me?" The frozen child climbed into the warm car.

"Where are you going?" President Lee asked.

"I'm going to the free picture show, where it's warm," the boy replied.

"Are you ready for Christmas?" he was asked.

"Oh, golly, Mister," began the answer, "we aren't going to have any Christmas at our house. Daddy died three months ago and left Mama and me and my little brother and sister."

Harold and the boy rode along in silence for a time. Then he turned up the heat in the car and at last saw that the child had stopped shivering and had relaxed a little. "Now, son," said President Lee, "give me your name and address. I promise you that somebody will come to your home and see that you *do* have a Christmas. You won't be forgotten."

The boy looked at the man, wanting to believe, but not sure how this stranger could promise him anything. However, he timidly gave his name and address, and as he got out of the car, he turned and said, "Oh, thanks, Mister."

President Lee waved good-bye. As the boy started to go toward the theater, he heard the man call, "Have a good time, son. It's almost Christmas Eve and it will be a good one for you!"

That evening as President Lee helped the bishops of his stake deliver food, clothing, and toys to the needy in the various wards, he remembered his promise to the little boy whom he had picked up earlier and given a ride into town. He asked one of the bishops to take some fuel and well-filled baskets to the little family, even though they were not part of his stake. At last, weary from no sleep the night before, he went to bed.

THINK ABOUT IT:

1. How do you think Harold's mother knew when her son was in danger?
2. Tell why you think Harold had a clear understanding of the true spirit of Christmas?
3. How did Harold's patriarchal blessing affect his life? What is a patriarchal blessing?

President Lee and his counselors developed a stake welfare program. It included a warehouse for storing food and other household items so that the needy would not go without the necessities of life. A stake gymnasium was built at much sacrifice so that recreational and educational opportunities, as well as heat and food, were available to his people.

The leaders of the Church became aware of what was happening in the Pioneer Stake, and in 1935 President Lee was called to work with others to expand and extend a welfare program throughout the Church.

Of this calling he said,

On April 2, 1935, I was called to the office of the First Presidency. My humble place in this [welfare] program at that time was described.

I left there about noontime and drove to the head of City Creek Canyon. I got out and walked up through the trees, where I sought my Heavenly Father. And I did receive a testimony, on that beautiful spring afternoon, that God had revealed the greatest organization that ever could be given to mankind, and that all that was needed now was that this organization be set to work, and the temporal welfare of the Latter-day Saints would be safe-guarded.

Six years later, on April 10, 1941, Harold B Lee was ordained an apostle by President Heber J. Grant. He served as a member of the Quorum of Twelve for the next thirty-one years.

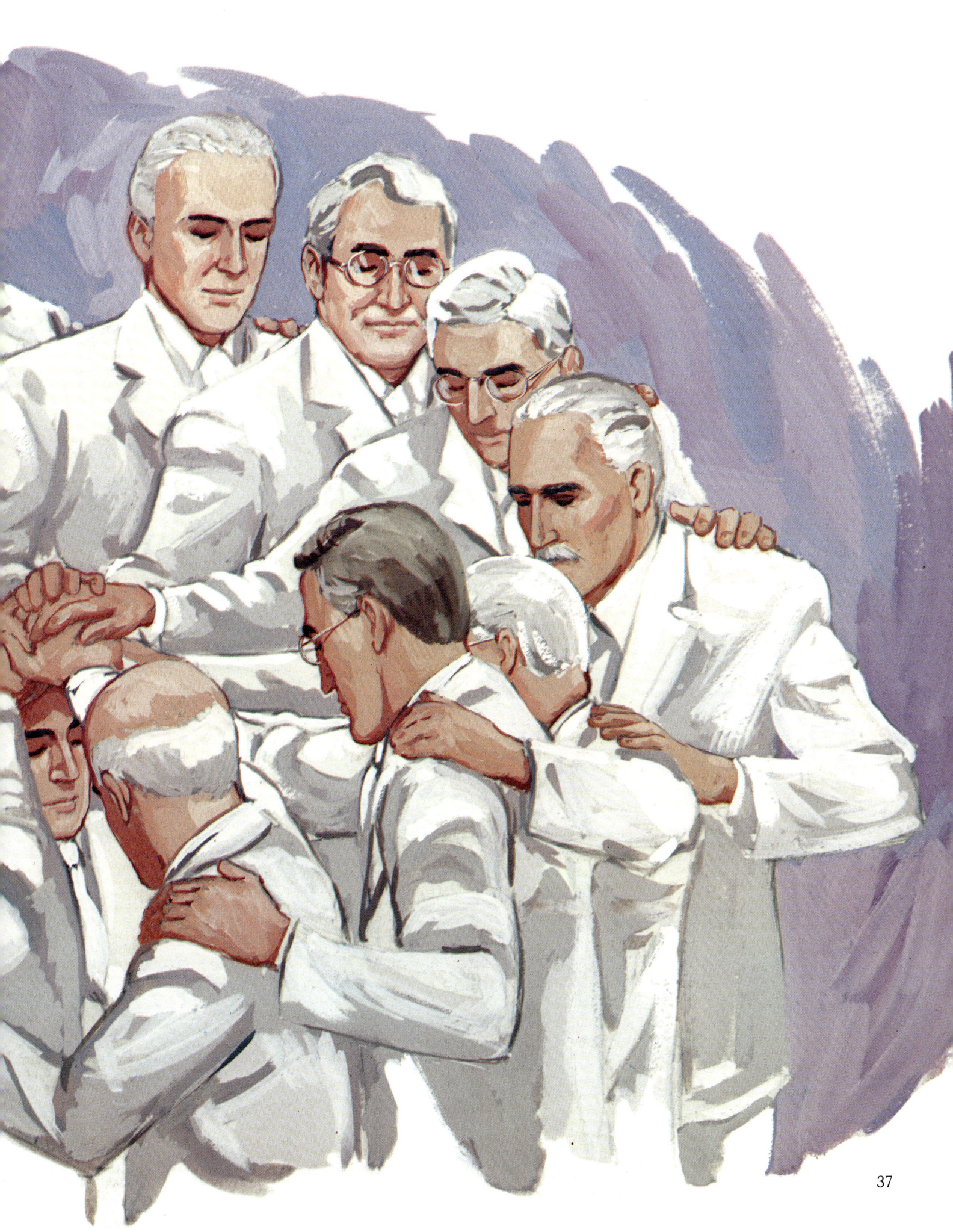

In telling of this call the next morning, he said,

> Since nine o'clock last night I have lived an entire lifetime in retrospect and in prospect. . . . Throughout the night, as I thought of this most appalling and soul-stirring assignment, there kept coming to me the words of the Apostle Paul, "Let us therefore come boldly unto the throne of grace, that we may obtain mercy, and find grace to help in time of need." . . . Therefore I shall take the word of the Apostle Paul. I shall come boldy unto the throne of grace and ask for mercy and his grace to help me in my time of need. With that help I cannot fail. Without it I cannot succeed.

On July 7, 1972, following the death of President Joseph Fielding Smith, Elder Lee was ordained as President of The Church of Jesus Christ of Latter-day Saints. A tribute made to him earlier by Elder Marion G. Romney concluded with this prophetic statement, "The future must reckon with Harold B. Lee." Elder Romney later served as President Lee's second counselor.

In 1962 Harold's wife, Fern, died. He had met her while on his mission in Denver some forty odd years before. They had been married in the Salt Lake Temple in 1923 and later had two lovely daughters. Fern's death brought much sorrow and loneliness to Harold. However, the following year on June 17, 1963, he married his second wife, Freda Joan Jensen, in the Salt Lake Temple.

Harold loved and appreciated his family. At his funeral President Gordon B. Hinckley spoke of him in these words:

> He was loyal to his family. I have heard him speak in hallowed affection of her who preceded him in death, the mother of his two children. I have listened with appreciation as he has spoken of her who has been his remarkable companion these past ten years—"My lovely Joan," as he called her.

On a cold Sabbath morning only a few weeks before President Lee's death on December 26, 1973, a woman sat in a Salt Lake City hospital outside the intensive care room, where her husband lay critically ill. Suddenly the quiet was broken by the sound of a nearby elevator stopping. The door opened and out stepped President and Sister Lee. They had learned of the hospitalization of this man, whose wife was keeping vigil, and had hurried to the hospital to offer any help they could.

President Lee gave the man a blessing, then quietly suggested that the wife stay with her husband "for a brief tender moment." He promised that he and Sister Lee would wait for her in the small lobby of that hospital unit.

A few minutes later when the woman went down the hall to join them, she saw President Lee talking to two little girls. President Lee's arm half encircled their young father, who was in a wheelchair trying to blow away the smoke from a lighted cigarette he was holding.

She stopped a few feet from this group to hear President Lee say to the girls, "You know your father loves you, and I'm sure you love him, whether or not he smokes." Then bending lower to the young man in the wheelchair, he said, "For your little girls and with the help of the Lord, you can do anything if you'll just remember who you are. Of course, you can stop smoking. I know you would go to the very gates of hell to help your loved ones, as I would mine. Now the Lord will bless you and the love of these sweet little daughters will help you, and soon you will be back at your sacrament meetings with them."

The man murmured a fervent, "Thank you. I'll try. I promise you and them, I'll try."

President Lee stooped over to give a gentle hug to each of the little girls. "You'll soon be together as a family, I'm sure," he said. Then with a loving smile, he left them and turned to greet the wife of the very ill man who was in the intensive care unit of the hospital. He promised her the strength needed to meet whatever came, reassured her that Heavenly Father cares about His children, and hurried off with Sister Lee for a long day of meetings and appointments.

The wife walked to the elevator with them and then, with a sigh, returned to the small lobby to renew her vigil. A hospital cleaning woman came to her chair. "Was that really President Lee?" the cleaning woman asked in a tone of reverence and amazement. When assured that it was, indeed, President Lee, she said, "He stopped and spoke to me. I told him that I was a Mormon and I knew I should be at Church instead of cleaning on the Sabbath day. He said, 'Someone has to take care of the sick.' And then I promised that I would go to Church later this afternoon. He thanked me for what I was doing and held out his hand to shake mine." Then in wonderment, she added, "I was blessed by a prophet—me—on a Sunday morning when I was in these old clothes doing my work! I'll never forget it."

The wife of the ill man nodded. "I know how you feel," she answered quietly. "I know!" As the cleaning woman hurried away, she thought, "Although everyone else is too busy, the prophet himself took time, unasked, to comfort a dying man and his wife, to encourage a straying father and give hope to his little girls, and to bless a cleaning woman. Truly he brought the light of the gospel into many lives today and will probably continue through a long busy day to bless countless others, too."

It may have reminded her of a statement President Lee had made shortly before:

> It is what you and I give to others that means more than all the sermons we preach. The lessons of our lives, the sermon of our own conduct and our own character will be most powerful in helping others . . . that person is happiest who forgets himself, and in the forgetting, climbs to the immortal memory of those whom he helped along the way.

THINK ABOUT IT:

1. Did President Lee seem to have a special love for poor and friendless people? Give reasons and examples for your answer.
2. Tell how you know that President Lee always honored his father and his mother.
3. What can we do to follow his example of "helping others along the way?"

President Lee deserves the immortal memory of many children and adults, for indeed, he helped many of them along the way!

It was at the funeral of President Harold B. Lee, only a few weeks after this incident in his life, that President Spencer W. Kimball summed up the feeling of the members of the Church and many others when he said, "A giant redwood has fallen and left a great space in the forest!"

President Lee left a fine example for each of us to remember and follow. He was a man of loyalty—loyalty to principle, country, family, and God.

TESTIMONY

I know full well the truth of what the Prophet Joseph told the early missionaries to Great Britain, that the nearer a person approaches the Lord, the greater power will be manifested by the adversary to prevent the accomplishment of His purposes. There is no shadow of doubt in my mind that these things are as certain today as in that day; but also, I am certain that, as the Lord said, "No weapon that is formed against you shall prosper. And that if a man lift his voice against His servants, as the Lord declared, he shall be confounded in his own due time." How grateful I am for your loyalty and your sustaining vote. I bear you solemn witness as to the divine mission of the Savior and the certainty as to His guiding hand in the affairs of His Church today, as in all dispensations of time. I know with a testimony more powerful than sight that, as the Lord declared, "The keys of the kingdom of God are committed unto man on the earth from the Prophet Joseph Smith to his successors down to the present. And from then shall the gospel roll forth unto the ends of the earth, as the stone which is cut out of the mountain without hands shall roll forth until it has filled the whole earth." Therefore, may the kingdom of God go forth, that the kingdom of heaven may come. I bear that testimony with all the convictions of my soul and leave my blessing upon the membership of the Church and the pure in heart everywhere in the name of the Lord, Jesus Christ. Amen.